# *Getting to know ...*
# *The Lake District*

Ron and Marlene Freethy

PRINTWISE PUBLICATIONS LIMITED

1992

This Edition
© Printwise Publications Ltd 1992

All photographs © Ron Freetny

Published by Printwise Publications Ltd
47 Bradshaw Road, Tottington, Bury, Lancs, BL8 3PW.

Warehouse and Orders
40-42 Willan Industrial Estate, Vere Street,
(off Eccles New Road),
Salford, M5 2GR.
Tel: 061-745 9168  Fax: 061-737 1755

ISBN No. 1 872226 47 7

Edited by

_liff Hayes_

Printed & bound by Manchester Free Press,
Paragon Mill, Jersey Street,
Manchester M4 6FP.
Tel: 061-236 8822

# Introduction and Acknowledgements

Some time ago we produced a small book describing the lakes which gave one of the most attractive areas in Britain its name. Since we planned this book the county boundaries have changed and instead of occupying parts of Lancashire, Cumberland and Westmorland we now have a new county of Cumbria. One of us was born in the Lake District and together we edited the magazine Pr*eview of Lakeland* which gave us a unique insight into the Lakes and we have been increasingly delighted with the way a balance has been achieved between tourism and wildlife. This present book is an update of our earlier work but most of the chapters have been extended to provide a useful guide for naturalists and historians. We have also used a combination of archive and modern photographs.

Whilst much of the material in the present book is new the present publishers have used some of the original illustrations, including Carole Pugh's line drawings and photographs by Bill Wilkinson, John Clegg and Michael Chesworth. Most of the modern photographs are, however, our own.

Thorneyholme May 1992

*Ron Freethy*

# About the Authors

Ron Freethy is President of the
North East Lancashire Rambler's
Association and has made many
television and radio programmes.
With his wife Marlene he has
written several walking books and
volumes on tourism throughout
the country. The couple live in the
Pendle area and are thus an ideal
choice to prepare this book and
the companion volumes.

*Marlene Freethy with
Bono ... always an
excuse for a walk*

# Contents

*A scene at Lakeside
on Windermere
photographed about
1950*

# Chapter one

# What are the Lakes?

The most famous, and at 866 square miles (1386 km) also the largest, of Britain's National Parks is so named because of seventeen stretches of fresh water left over from the Ice Ages. These ended around 15,000 years ago and the lakes are only transitory puddles which have been declining in size ever since they were formed. Fast flowing streams and rivers have remorselessly chiselled away at the lakes and shifted pebbles and silt from the foot of each lake to its head. At Buttermere and Derwentwater the filling in process can be seen in the form of small deltas but the two ancient lake beds can still be detected especially if viewed from a height. The now dry Kentmere, above Kendal, has been a valuable quarry for diatomite so called from the organisms which once abounded in the shallowing waters when the climate of Britain was warmer than at the present time. Diatomite is a white silica-rich material which can be ground to a powder which is so resistant to heat that it is used in the production of fireproof cements, as an absorbent material in the manufacture of explosives and of course as an insulator. All the shallow lakes of the area are rich in diatoms and in time will produce diatomite when the standing waters have evaporated and stand no more.

The lakes have been ground out of some of the world's most ancient rocks. Geologists inform us that some of the slaty rocks of Skiddaw above Keswick-on-Derwentwater are 530 million years old. The rocks around Borrowdale are 500 million years old and formed of lava and ash which spewed out of massive volcanoes whilst the Silurian slates which are found around Windermere are the youngest rocks in the area and are only around 420 million years old. Only 420 million indeed!

But the geological features which give the area its name are the lakes themselves. How many are there? Apart from the many small tarns there are some 17 stretches of water large enough to be called lakes, some easily accessible and often abounding with visitors in the high season. Windermere, Ullswater, Derwentwater and Coniston all soak up the summer flood of humanity easily but have varying numbers of secluded spots which would still be recognised by Wordsworth, Southey, Coleridge and the rest of the distinguished band of Lakeland's poets. Other lakes such as Thirlmere have been dammed (some would say damned!) to provide water for thirsty areas around Manchester.

The banks have been planted up with trees, but recently walks have been opened up through the conifers to reveal a backdrop of splendidly savage scenery. Ennerdale and Wastwater are sill clear unpolluted lakes on which surprisingly souless city planners in search of cheap water have recently focussed their unwelcome attention. The only sensible approach to water shortage is to stop wasting so much of it!

No account of the waters of the Lake District would be complete without reference to the man-made Tarn Hows. The rest of this book will therefore describe the 17 natural waters laid out in the table plus Tarn Hows.

| Table of English Lakes  1 mile = 1.61 km   1 foot = 0.31 metres | | | |
|---|---|---|---|
| Lake | Max length miles | Max breadth miles | Max depth feet |
| Windermere | 10.5 | 1.25 | 219 |
| Ullswater | 7.5 | 0.75 | 205 |
| Coniston | 5.25 | 0.5 | 184 |
| Bassenthwaite | 4.0 | 0.75 | 70 |
| Thirlmere | 3.8 | 0.5 | 158 |
| Haweswater | 4.0 | 0.5 | 198 |
| Derwentwater | 3.5 | 1.25 | 72 |
| Crummock | 3.5 | 0.8 | 144 |
| Wastwater | 3.0 | 0.5 | 258 |
| Ennerdale | 2.5 | 0.75 | 148 |
| Esthwaite | 1.5 | 0.5 | 80 |
| Buttermere | 1.25 | 0.8 | 94 |
| Loweswater | 1.25 | 0.8 | 60 |
| Grasmere | 1.0 | 0.5 | 75 |
| Rydal Water | 0.75 | 0.25 | 55 |
| Brother's Water | 0.4 | 0.25 | 70 |
| Elterwater | 0.4 | irregular | 70 |

# Chapter Two

# *Windermere*

The most nostalgic way to approach England's largest lake is on board the steam train which runs from Haverthwaite to the pier at Lakeside. The track follows the line of the River Leven from its estuary at Greenodd to its beginnings at the point where it flows out of Windermere. The short but now beautiful river was once heavily industrialised and had iron foundries, a dolly blue works, gunpowder factories and other timber-dependent industries set at short intervals along its banks. Despite these activities the Leven retained its reputation as a fine salmon river. All the industries have now gone; the old blast furnaces are crumbling away behind a screen of fine trees including oak and ash; the blue works has now been converted into an exclusive holiday complex; the old bobbin mill at Stott park is now a fascinating working museum situated close to Newby Bridge. Salmon can still be seen powering their way under the arches of the bridge near the Swan Hotel and also further downstream at Lowood Bridge at Haverthwaite.

Not so long ago otters, thought to be a menace to fish stocks, were hunted by men on foot with their baying hounds and strident horns. Deer still wander the woodlands and both roe and small herds of red deer, Britian's largest land mammal, are

*Cumbria, one of the locomotives gets up steam ready for its journey along the Leven Valley from Haverthwaite to Lakeside*

frequently observed.

Being large and easily reached by millions of day trippers travelling along the nearby M6 motorway, the lake can be crowded in the summer especially at weekends. The water was used at least from the time of the Romans, whose fort at Galava was ideally sited at the foot of the lake along which building stone was ferried. All traces of the Roman occupation have now gone, swamped beneath the hotels and poured concrete car parks at Waterhead. During the industrial heyday of Lakeland, Windermere was used to transport both raw materials and finished goods particularly charcoal, gunpowder and iron ore. Industrialists built their mansions overlooking the most attractive bays, and many are still in private hands thus restricting access to a great expanse of the eastern shoreline of the lake. One such structure, now the Belsfield Hotel overlooking Bowness Bay, was the home of William Schneider who travelled daily to his business interests in the fast developing iron and ship-building town at Barrow-in-Furness. Apparently Schneider walked from Belsfield accompanied by his butler, carrying his breakfast

*William Schneider's steam yacht is now kept at the Steam Museum and is occasionally seen on Windermere*

13

*Schneider and his butler outside the Belsfield prepare to take breakfast and the morning mail down to the Esperance on the lake*

on a silver tray down to the pier where his steam yacht Es*perance* waited and bobbed gently on the lapping water. Attending to his mail on the lake journey to Lakeside he then completed his journey to Barrow by steam train. This journey can be followed, in part at least, by visitors joining a tour known as 'The Lakeland Link' which instead of going to Barrow ends its steam journey at the Haverthwaite terminus. The circle back to Bowness is occasionally completed in a 1920s Leyland bus which makes

a detour to Holker Hall, home of the Cavendish family who were friends of Mr Schneider. Holker is now open to the public, has a motor museum, a fine herd of deer and often holds rallies of hot air balloonists. The *Esperance* is still in working order and can be viewed at the Steamboat Museum at Bowness. Whilst we were editing *Preview of Lakeland* we visited the Steamboat Museum on June 30th 1990 to witness the inauguration of the Arthur Ransome Society. Ransome made Lakeland famous by means of his childrens' book *Swallows and Amazons*. The society is based at the 'Museum of Lakeland Life in Kendal' as well as at the Steamboat Museum, the former having many of the writer's personal possessions on display. We learned much of the life of Ransome from our mountaineering friend and Lakeland enthusiast, Dudley Green. Arthur Mitchell Ransome was born in Leeds on 18 January, 1884, the eldest son of Cyril Ransome, professor of History at the Yorkshire College which later became Leeds University. Many childhood holidays were spent in the Lake District and the boy loved mingling with the charcoal burners, and was even allowed on one occasion to take a turn at the wheel of the steam yacht *Gondola* on Coniston which has been restored and described in chapter four. Arthur was sent to Prep. School at Windermere and although he did not enjoy the school itself he loved to be close to the lake and wrote in later years of the great frost of 1896. At this time the boys skated on the lake and watched local folk drive their carriages onto the ice. In 1897 his father died but Arthur's mother supervised his education first at Rugby and then as he read science at Leeds college. The young man, however, was set

*The Belsfield Hotel, former home of William Schneider viewed from the surface of Windermere*

*One of Holker Hall's wonderful old cars shown to its best advantage with the delightful residence in the background*

16

upon a writing career and retained an everlasting love of the Lake District, spending some time based at Coniston walking, writing, and making friends with the Collingwood family who were later delighted to be incorporated into his childrens' novels. In 1909 Arthur married Ivy Walker whom he met in London, but by 1913 both had realised that they were unsuited and they drifted apart. Arthur went to Russia intending to collect and adapt a volume of folk tales. He remained in Russia during the First World War and earned a reputation as a skilled journalist working for the Daily News, a paper with strong liberal sympathies.

When the Revolution started in March 1917 Ransome was in Petrograd and got to know Trotsky, Lenin and other influential leaders. He also fell in love with Trotsky's secretary Eugenia Petrovna Shelepina and in 1924 obtained a divorce and the couple married. They returned to England and bought a cottage in the Winster Valley, and Arthur continued to write influential political articles and was by now working for the Guardian.

Had it not been for renewing his friendship with the Collingwoods, Ransome would not have been

*Holker Hall photographed around 1900*

remembered as a writer for who celebrates political journalists when the events they recorded lie forgotten on the dusty pages of history? Dora Collingwood married Ernest Altounyan in 1915 and after a period working in Syria the family, now consisting of five children, returned to the lakes. Arthur taught the children Taqui, Susie, Mavis, Roger and Brigit to sail. He dedicated *Swallows and Amazons* to the children, the book being published in 1930. It was Brigit who proudly spoke at the opening of the Arthur Ransome society and unveiled the restored family boat which is now on display.

Between 1930 and his death on 3rd June 1967 Arthur Ransome became a distinguished literary figure moving occasionally to London to satisfy his wife, she in turn agreeing to return to the Lake District to humour her husband's love of the area and its fishing, which was a religion with him. He is buried in Rusland church, a beautiful Lakeland area which he loved in life and no doubt rests in peace.

Since 1969, yet another former mansion, once owned by a Manchester businessman, has been the headquarters of the Lake District National Park. Brockholes – meaning a place where badgers lived – is situated between Windermere and Ambleside on the A591. Magnificent woodland walks lead out from the neat formalised gardens and are full of bird song with chiff-chaff, great tit and the thrush family being prominent. Views over the lake towards the jagged peaks of the Langdales are as fine as any in Lakeland and several species of waterfowl make good use of the sheltered bay. The woodland is rich in common flowers including yellow flag with the occasional rarity such as globe flower. In wet weather visitors can enjoy the well prepared audio-visual presentation and stroll around expertly ordered displays depicting lakeland wildlife, history, farming and industry. There is also a bookshop, and a large refreshment area. The splendour of Windermere has not been lost, even on the more populated eastern shore, but the real essence of its beauty can best be appreciated from the west bank which is criss-crossed with flower-strewn footpaths each a strong candidate in a scenic beauty competition which can have only

*The restored Sunderland Flying Boat visiting Windermere in 1990*

one winner – the tourist with time to stop and stare.

Between Bowness and Lakeside the lake is crossed by a chain ferry carrying foot passengers and cars across to Ferry House, once a hotel, but now the headquarters of the Freshwater Biological Association whose scientists keep a constant check on the fauna and flora of the aquatic life throughout Lakeland. Windermere's most fascinating fish is the char which although quite common, requires a patient and skillful angler to catch it. It is certainly worth the effort because potted char is a real tasty dish. It lives deep down in the cold water and had its origins in the coastal areas around the Arctic and the rivers flowing into it. In Britain and other countries such as Sweden, North America, Greenland and Iceland char were stranded following the Ice Ages and have survived in deep lakes but have been landlocked ever since and have lost their once strong migratory urge.

There is obviously no way the char from the various lakes can come into contact so each population may well be evolving into a species unique to each particular lake.

We remember as youngsters learning to row on Windermere, making sure to keep close to the edge to avoid the steamers, Teal, Swan, Cygnet, Tern and Swift. We soon learned that the first two were much larger and created a very alarming wash. Competence comes with ambition, and we were soon easing our way into quiet bays and around tiny islands. No lakeland island has more beauty and history than the romantic sounding, 38 acre, Belle Island which in the 14th century was called Great Holme. During the Civil War of the 1640s the loyal Phillipson family held their island for the King for 80 days against the forces of Parliament before being overcome. In 1774 a wealthy man by the name of English employed the architect John Plaw to design a unique circular house with views in all directions through the trees and over the water. Soon after its completion the house with its classical looking portico was sold to the Curwen family. It is thought that it was the beauty of Isabella Curwen

*Another view of the vessels on display at the Windermere Boat Museum*

*The otter, although not so common these days, is still a resident around Windermere and the River Leven*

which was the reason for the change of name to Belle Isle. The Curwens still live on the site, the largest and the only one of seventeen islands on Windermere to be occupied. Our childhood love of Windermere's islands was shared by Wordsworth who was at school at Hawkshead and wrote

> *"It was the pastime of our afternoons*
> *To beat along the plain of Windermere*
> *With rival oars, and the selected bourne*
> *Was now an Island musical with birds*
> *That sang for ever; now a Sister Isle*
> *Beneath the oak's umbrageous covert sown*
> *With lilies of the valley like a field."*

The Wordsworth family had an interest in rowing and in 1826 William's nephew was a member of the Cambridge crew in the first boat race.

Yet another magnificent dwelling and estate put to good use is at Fell Foot opposite the steamer terminus and railway station at Lakeside. What a fascinating tale Fell Foot has to tell from its building by the Robinson family in the early years of the 18th century. Jeremiah Dixon, a Leeds businessman and the son-in-law of John Smeaton the designer of the Eddystone lighthouse, purchased the estate in 1774, but his descendants sold out in 1859 to Colonel Ridehalgh. The colonel was clearly in the mould of Victorian eccentrics' full of ability and energy.

One of the founders of the Royal Windermere Yacht Club, Ridehalgh built a small dockyard, made his own coal gas and had a line of gas lamps dotted along the lakeside which must have been the wonder of the age to the locals. Trees and bushes, especially rhododendrons were planted and the Colonel even had his own pack of hounds which he often transported by steam boat to hunt the fox at the Ambleside end of the lake. What a noise they must have made in transit and what a problem they must have been for the huntsman! On the death of Colonel Ridehalgh the estate was sold to Oswald Hedley whose grand

*The Arctic char is one of Lakeland's most fascinating fish and a "left-over" species from the Ice Ages*

*The old blast furnaces at Backbarrow are now being swallowed by trees, but are an important part of Lakeland's industrial history*

24

designs never materialised. In 1906 he demolished the old house but only the foundations of its replacement had been established when Mrs Hedley died and Oswald moved up the lake to Calgarth Hall which is now an outdoor pursuit centre. Fell Foot was left to disappear beneath a tangle of vegetation until it was taken over by the National Trust in 1948. After a 21 year stint as a caravan site, the 18 acre site has been laid out as a Country Park. As you park your car spare a thought for the ill-fated Hedley family because you are standing on the foundations of their intended house. If you take refreshment in the cafe you are sitting over one of the Colonel Ridehalgh's favourite spots.

Despite the effects of industry and tourism Windermere, especially along the western shore, has many reed fringed bays and a number of islands which are ideal bird sanctuaries. During the cold periods of winter, providing stretches of water remain open, flocks of up to 300 goldeneye may be seen with large flocks of tufted duck and pochard plus a group of up to 60 whooper swans. The area opposite Wray castle is particularly popular,

*A busy scene at Waterhead, near Ambleside*

but when areas of the lake begin to freeze over the stretch served by the chain ferry near the headquarters of the Freshwater Biological Association remains open and large numbers of wildfowl and gulls accumulate. Other species recorded include red breasted merganser, goosander, shelduck plus little and great crested grebe with the occasional rarity such as the Slavonian grebe. Both greylag and Canada geese breed around the fringes of the lake with the population of the latter species rising steadily. Cormorants can be seen along the length of the lake but are more common in winter when as many as 200 may be seen roosting around Roughholme Island. In the bay below Millers Ground is a large gull roost mainly of black headed, herring and lesser black backed gulls, but it is always worth examining each bird in search of great black backed, common, Mediterranean and little gulls and in rough weather the kittiwake. Terns

also frequent Windermere the most regular visitors being common and sandwich but arctic, caspian, little and black terns have all been recorded occasionally. Belle Island with its famous round house surrounded by trees, and mentioned above, can be visited during the summer and woodland species recorded here include pied flycatcher, wood warbler, blackcap, great spotted and green woodpecker and which all breed as do sparrowhawk and tawny owl. In the damp areas there are breeding woodcock, snipe and redshank whilst sightings of buzzards are becoming increasingly common. The nightjar, however, is declining. Other woodlands close to the lake are Cunsey Woods and Grizedale which is described in chapter twelve. Good birdwatching, however, is guaranteed by visiting the summer tourist traps during the winter months.

**Access**

Windermere's eastern shore is followed by the A592 almost into Bowness and then by the A591 as far as Waterhead. Almost at the head of the lake is Brockhole, the National Park Information Centre from which run a number of paths towards the

*During the 1930s and early 1940s Sunderland Flying Boats were constructed by Short Brothers on the shores of Windermere*

*The authors prepare to explore Lakeland by balloon from the Lowood Hotel on the shores of Windermere. The balloon was piloted by Bob Jones*

river. Many passerines including the rare hawfinch have been recorded here. Apart from the tourist centres there are few areas open to the public along the eastern side. The western side of the lake leads from Newby Bridge (signed off the A590) to Skelwith Bridge, and from these are some footpaths and excellent viewpoints. There is interesting bird watching from both sides of the ferry between Far Sawrey and Bowness and from off the ferry itself which carries cars and passengers, the journey taking between five and ten minutes.

We are absolutely convinced that Windermere is underused by naturalists because they cannot see beyond the crowds at Lakeside, Bowness, Windermere and Waterhead near Ambleside. There are quiet places just as there always have been even during the Second World War when perch were being netted and tinned to feed a hungry population and flying boats were being constructed and tested on the

*A view of the countryside around Windermere from Bob Jones' balloon*

29

banks of the Lake. In late 1990 memories of the past were revived by a restored Sunderland flying boat landing on the lake and how graceful she looked, the last in a distinguished line.

The best way to realise how much of the bank is still 'natural' is to take a trip in a hot air balloon which we did on a warm summer evening. Laid out below us like a map were the green fields, green hedgerows, the silver ribbons of the lakes and the numerous tarns looking just like tears – indeed the Norse word for a tear is actually tarn.

Like Windermere, Ullswater is also busy during the peak holiday season but there are even more secret places where it is possible to be alone with nature.

*Chapter Three*

# *Ullswater:*
## *The Vikings' Lake*

A gusting early April breeze swept down from the snow capped summit of Helvellyn and the lower, but still substantial slopes of Dolywaggon, Fairfield and Place Fell. Despite the apparent severity, spring seems to come early to the National Trust owned woodlands which fringe Ullswater. Wordsworth often walked here with his sister Dorothy and is said to have been enchanted by the carpets of small delicate wild daffodils which thrive in the damp soil beneath the gnarled old oaks and majestic birches. On daffodil days with the lake kissed by the morning sun we always feel at one with Wordsworth when he wrote

Wild daffodils
growing on the
breezy shores of
Ullswater still
"dance" as they did
when they inspired
Dorothy
Wordsworth's prose
and William's poem

"I wandered lonely as a cloud
That floats on high o'er vales and hills
When all at once I saw a crowd,
A host of golden daffodils;
Beside the lake, beneath the trees
Fluttering and dancing in the breeze

Continuous as the stars that shine
And twinkle on the milky way,
They stretched in never ending line
Along the margin of a bay:
Ten thousand saw I at a glance
Tossing their heads in sprightly dance.

The waves beside them danced; but they
Out-did the sparkling waves in glee
A poet could not but be gay,
In such jocund company:
I gazed – and gazed – but little thought
What wealth to me the show had brought.

For oft, when on my couch I lie
In vacant or in pensive mood,
They flash upon that inward eye
Which is the bliss of solitude;
And then my heart with pleasure fills
And dances with the daffodils."

We make no excuse for quoting this poem in full because we feel that everyone should read it in the context in which it was written.

Ullswater is around 7 miles long, almost a mile across at its widest point, and is thus Lakeland's second largest stretch of water, after Windermere. It lacks the latter's hustle and bustle, however, and retains a calm serenity which ensures its continued affection in the hearts of those who wish to stroll in the woods and enjoy the bracing air of the lakeside settlements of Pooley Bridge, Howtown and Glenridding.

Howtown can be reached along a cul-de-sac road from Pooley Bridge, but the main road from the same spot to Glenridding is a delight. Gentle rises, sharp but

33

*The cinnabar moth
larvae feeding upon
the flowers of ragwort*

comparatively safe bends and plenty of laybys with panoramic views up the lake make this one of Cumbria's most spectacular routes. Although it can be busy at peak periods it is often surprisingly quiet and depending upon the season there are banks of primrose, cow parsley, red campion and the gloriously golden blooms of ragwort. What a pity that this plant is so poisonous to cattle for it really is a joy to behold and is always attractive to moths such as the cinnabar which lays its eggs upon it. Both the adult insect and the caterpillar are unpleasant to eat – indeed they are poisonous since they contain traces of cyanide. The adults are black and red whilst the black and yellow caterpillars are also conspicuous. These combinations act as warning colours

34

and inform potential predators that danger threatens. Insects with stings such as wasps also advertise their presence by having warning colours. Some scientists believe that the insect may extract its poison from the ragwort which may explain why the plant can be fatal to cattle and especially to horses.

Ulf was a Viking leader and Ulverston and Ulpha both suggest that he had control over a wide area since Ulfswater – now Ullswater – was also in his domain. The lake is a 'public highway' and as such anyone is able to launch a boat without fee and cruise into its many sheltered bays. Peace and safety are assured, however, by the presence of organised lake wardens and for those without the desire to propel themselves a regular ferry service circles the lake taking about an hour to call at Pooley Bridge, Howtown and Glenridding. The journey can be broken at any point and it is far the best way to get to know both the lake and settlements huddled along its shore, all of which have a distinctly nautical air.

The name Pooley Bridge means the pool by the hill and the settlement developed at the point where the River Eamont meets Ullswater. The Eamont, like many Lake District rivers is a substantial waterway, but tends to be overshadowed by the lakes. In the centre of Pooley Bridge is St Paul's church which although attractive is not ancient and only dates to 1868. Prior to this the villagers had to walk to St Michael's at Barton which is 2 miles along the road towards Penrith. This lovely building was erected in 1150 but substantial additions were made between 1318 and 1536 when it was administered by the canons of Wartre Priory, an Augustinian establishment near York. William Wordsworth's grandfather, Richard, is buried in the churchyard and close by are the graves of his grandson and two of his aunts.

Howtown is anything but a town, being a lovely hamlet at the end of a narrow twisting road from Pooley Bridge. The best way to appreciate the spread of tiny cottages and farms is to allow yourself the luxury of a boat trip on the M.V. Raven from Glenridding pier where there is ample car parking and then to return from Howtown along well marked paths through a tangle of flowery woodlands. In spring, woodpeckers drum, chaffinches seem to be everywhere and red squirrels leap among the trees which include ancient and gnarled as well as supple young ashes. The head of the lake is at Patterdale – the dale of St Patrick – and once a holy spot. Some of the Celtic Saint's healing powers are

*The red-breasted merganser and her ducklings set sail along Ullswater*

supposed to remain in the spring water of St Patrick's well close by the boat landing at Glenridding.

One magnificently warm day in early June we watched a duck red-breasted merganser sailing majestically in Glenridding bay with 13 ducklings behind her like old wooden ships of the line in battle order. The species is rapidly expanding its breeding range and some 3,000 pairs now nest in Britain. The male is a splendid bird with a bottle green head, whilst his mate has a chestnut crown and like the rest of the saw-billed ducks they are fish eaters. The prey is captured after an underwater pursuit and the inner surface of the bird's bill has serrations like the teeth of a saw, each sharp point sloping backwards so that the more the fish struggles the more firmly it is held. Mergansers need open water to feed and trees under which they nest although they sometimes even lay their clutch high up within a hollow trunk. Strangely enough many ducks choose hollow trees as nest sites and it is even more strange to see one day old, only recently dry, chicks launching themselves into space and landing literally as gently as a feather before following their mother to the nearest water. Here they soon learn to dive for water crustaceans and insects which abound in the lake, and later they learn to catch fish. There is little chance of Ullswater running short of water since streams from the mighty hills enclosing it cascade into it after pouring over stony beds and waterfalls including the famous Aira Force which is reached by footpath from a car park near Glenridding. The stream drops in a deafening clatter over a 70 foot (21 metre) wall of sheer rock on its way from Martindale Common to the lake. Another attractive stream drains from Helvellyn into Red Tarn and then becomes Glenridding Beck before entering Ullswater. Now a delightfully healthy stream full of stonefly and mayfly larvae, and therefore also a favoured haunt of

*The waterfalls around Ullswater are at their best during rain*

all the year round dippers and summer visiting common sandpipers, the beck once drained Greenside lead mines. The last of these closed in 1962 bringing to a close more than three centuries of hard and dangerous toil. Few anglers, however, will mourn its passing since the pollutants it produced had much to do with reduction of Ullswater's char fishery. It also adversely affected a fish called the coregonus or schelly which is unique to the lake. Although related to the herring the latter is, like the char, which is of the salmon family, an example of a once migratory fish cut off from the sea by drift deposited by melting glaciers as the Ice Age ground to a finish. The now isolated fish populations – and no doubt other aquatic creatures if scientists had the time to search –inter-breed to produce new and therefore unique variants. There are signs that now the mines have closed the future of both the coregonus and the Ullswater char are more certain. For a time after the mines had closed, muffled underground explosions reverberated around the lonely hillsides. Sensitive instruments were being tested in a government sponsored effort to produce a machine which could be used in the

*A misty morning view over Ullswater*

1960s to detect distant underground nuclear explosions being tested by foreign powers.

Ullswater brings to mind bird song and banks of flowers, the gentle chug of the ferry vessel Raven the calling of ewes to their lambs, soaring larks and sweet smelling grasses. Tumbling waters of the uplands mingle their tune with the rutting calls of the red deer which thrive on the fells of Martindale. In winter the lakeside woodlands provide shelter from the icy blasts and this is truly a lake for all seasons.

Being quite deep, Ullswater is not particularly food rich. The cool clear water is therefore used more as a roost than a feeding station but bays around Pooley bridge, Howtown and Glenridding can hold flocks of up to 100 each of mallard, pochard and tufted with a few goldeneye and red breasted merganser and goosander. In winter great crested and little grebe both occur and pollution from the lead mines has cleared remarkably quickly and already the stream has substantial populations of stonefly, mayfly and dragonfly larvae. These are fed upon by dipper, grey wagtail and common sandpiper. The three species do not feed in the same manner and therefore are not in direct competition. The reduction in lead pollution has also meant the increase in the flocks of freshwater duck frequenting Glenridding Bay.

**Access**

Take junction 40 off the M6 and then the A66 towards Keswick but almost immediately turning left into the A592 which follows the western bank of the lake. National Trust woodlands at Gowbarrow Park and to Aira Force are open at all times. There is a car park with toilets and a cafe. A cul-de-sac leads from Pooley Bridge to Howtown on the east bank. A steamer service operates between Glenridding, Howtown and Pooley Bridge where the River Eamont enters the lake with sufficient force to keep the water open even in cold weather.

*Chapter Four*

# *Coniston*

*Coniston Lake around 1900*

Watched over by its benevolent Old Man, Coniston well deserves its place as one of Lakeland's 'tourist traps'. As with most of Lakeland the fierce Norsemen stamped their authority on the area, the lake being known for centuries as Thurston's water. Soon after the Norman Conquest came the monastic system and many areas, including Lakeland came under the sway of the mighty Abbeys. In the 13th century the monks of Furness had fishing rights on the lake and were allowed to use one boat and twenty nets whilst William de Lancaster also had the right to fish. It was the monks, however, who brought industry to

*The grayling is underrated as a game fish and those anglers who know it rate it with the salmon as a fighting fish*

Arthur Ransome gives us a vivid picture of charcoal burning when "A great wood ran up the hillside on the eastern shore of the lake – far up it they could see smoke curling slowly above the trees, a thin trickle of smoke climbing straight up."

As children we remember being taken to see a charcoal burner appropriately called Ashburner at work and following his family tradition dating back to the 17th century. Charcoal can be produced from any species of tree but in the Lake District oak, ash and birch were the ones most frequently used. The cutting was carried out during the spring and the timber stacked until autumn when it was dry enough for the burn to begin. A pitstead was begun by levelling a circle about 60 feet (almost 20 metres) in diameter and a central stake called a Motty Peg hammered into the ground. The rest of the timber was then skillfully stacked around and against this 'central peg'. The whole idea was to burn the wood in a restricted air supply so the wood was covered in a layer of grass and reeds with any holes sealed with a fine sub-soil which they called 'sammel'. The central peg was then removed and a lighted taper dropped in and then the top was resealed with a sod. As the charcoal formed, the pitstead tended to shrink and holes develop

the area when they found rich deposits of iron ore close to the lake. Trees were felled to produce the charcoal required for smelting and soon smoke curled into the air and bloomeries were a feature of each of the many clearings. Charcoal burning was a feature of Lakeland for many centuries and was still going on regularly as late as the 1930s. In *Swallows and Amazons*,

which would have allowed air to enter and the result would have been a mammoth bonfire and no charcoal. At the end of the burn the pitstead was slaked with water and the charcoal bagged ready for market. It would probably have been moved by boat to the Torver end of the lake and thence along the valley of the River Crake which drains Coniston and reaches the sea at the old port of Greenodd. This is an excellent fishing river and supports salmon, trout and the often underrated grayling which is a brave fighting fish and with an excellent taste.

Coniston also had other industries in addition to charcoal burning and the water of the lake is cold enough to support char and there are also good stocks of trout, perch and pike and all of these species are more plentiful now than in times past. As at Ullswater the reason is not far to seek. Many of the local streams tumbling down over their stony beds from the steep hillsides were once

*Charcoal burning was a feature of Lakeland life until the 1930s*

*The River Crake flowing into the sea at Greenodd*

used to power mine machinery. Not only was there the iron which the monks exploited but there were also vast deposits of copper which were extensively worked from the time of Elizabeth I. This enterprise polluted the feeder streams to such an extent that Coniston lake as a fishery almost died. Anyone seeking to climb the Old Man must pass through Coppermines Valley which is honeycombed with the old workings which were still yielding ore up to the middle of the

nineteenth century. Once the mines closed, the lake as a fishery began to improve and now there is excellent sport to be had upon the tranquil waters only occasionally disturbed by a yacht. Once steamers plied the lake providing locals with a ferry and visitors with an "exhilarating perambulation of Thurston's enchantingly sculptured coastline". *The Lady of the Lake* and the *Gondola* competed for custom but by 1939 both graceful vessels had been abandoned and lay neglected for many years. *The Lady of the Lake* was unfortunately broken up in 1950 but *Gondola* slept on, half submerged in the reeds around the lake edge, with only grebes, moorhens and wildfowl for company. Fortunately the story has a happy ending for the *Gondola* was restored to all her former glory and since 1983 she has ferried tourists around the lake. Her maiden voyage was graced by the presence of the grandchildren and great grandchildren of her old skipper, Captain Hamill, who navigated her through these waters for over 50 years. We love to travel on *Gondola* as she is a reminder of Victorian elegance – all polished brass and wood.

Coniston has seen boats travelling much faster than the *Gondola* for it was here that Donald Campbell raced his speedboat *Bluebird* and was reaching record-breaking speed when she apparently struck a log, somersaulted and Campbell's body was never recovered despite a diligent search. Even in winter optimistic divers still plumb the depths of Coniston, do doubt hoping to dredge up some piece of the ill-fated *Bluebird,*

Campbell, the fearless 20th century adventurer, was a complete contrast

*The old landing stage for the Gondola at the Crake end of Coniston Lake*

to John Ruskin the 19th century scholar who made his home at Brantwood and enjoyed the views from the lovely house. Perhaps 'enjoyed' is too strong a word for Ruskin who certainly did not have a sunny disposition. Perhaps we should say that he was happier here than he would have been anywhere else on earth and there is no finer compliment than that. Brantwood was home to Ruskin for the last 29 years of his life prior to his death in 1900. It has been beautifully restored and is open daily in summer and from Wednesday to Sunday in winter. Nature trails have been laid out through the grounds with attractive views out over the lake at all times of the year but particularly in autumn when the blood red setting sun is reflected in the water. This is one of our favourite museums anywhere in the country.

Coniston is, in our opinion, an excellent centre for birdwatching, as much of its shore is strewn with

*Brantwood is one of the best organised literary museums in the country*

*Hound trailing and fox hunting is as much a religion as a sport in the Lake District and the dogs are exercised whatever the weather*

pebbles – dippers and grey wagtails are therefore able to frequent the edge of the lake. Other breeding birds along the fringe include great crested grebe plus a Slavonian grebe recorded in November 1977, common sandpiper, coot and moorhen. Although Coniston is not regarded as a major ornithological site compared to many of the other lakes there can be as many as 400 greylag geese present during the winter months and it can provide days of rare excitement and should not be ignored. At Nibthwaite there is a roost of cormorants which can exceed 50 individuals at times and especially during February and early March there can be flocks of mallard and pochard containing more than 500 birds with lesser, but still impressive numbers of goldeneye, goosander, merganser, whooper, Bewick and mute swans with greylag and Canada geese both regular visitors with a few pairs of the latter breeding close by. We once enjoyed a couple of hours on a late May

*Coniston village photographed from the church tower around 1910*

in these woodlands but in winter their numbers are swelled and often the flocks are accompanied by brambling which breed in Scandinavia. All three British woodpeckers breed on the wooded slopes overlooking the lake.

**Access**

In contrast to Windermere a great deal of Coniston's lakeside especially on the Eastern side, is freely open to the public and many laybys and parking areas overlook the lake or are set back among the trees. Coniston can be reached from Greenodd via the A5084, the A593 from Ambleside or the A5285 from Hawkshead.

morning watching an osprey hunt for fish and diving several times with a terrific splash in pursuit of fish. Their talons have rough hooks on them which help them to grip their prey. High above the lake on Dow Cragg and the soaring cliffs of Coniston Old Man, raven and peregrine have bred successfully for many years whilst in the tree lined lower valleys buzzard and sparrowhawk are both increasing in numbers following almost catstrophic declines during the 1960s. Their decline was due to the use of poisonous agricultural chemicals. The chaffinch is resident

# Chapter Five

# *Bassenthwaite*

The banning of motorboats gives Bassenthwaite a tranquillity appreciated by naturalists, anglers and those who like messing about in boats propelled by wind or oar. Access to the lake shore is restricted but there are excellent views across it of Skiddaw. The dual carriageway A66 runs alongside the lake and a few parking places allow views into sheltered bays which abound with wildfowl particularly tufted duck, pochard and mallard but there are often goosander and goldeneye in winter. The very best bird watching area along the whole four mile length of the lake is at the layby close to Ouse Bridge at the north end. At the southern end of the lake is an extensive area of fen which often attracts waders such as snipe and redshank. Buzzard and sparrowhawk are frequent in the surrounding woodlands whilst the lucky watcher can sometimes catch a glimpse of a soaring golden eagle. In winter when the sun begins to set and the temperature falls huge numbers of black headed and common gulls drop in for their nightly roost.

Although its 70 feet (21 metres) depth is not sufficient to encourage the char which likes deep cold water, the vendace, another example of a landlocked fish does occur here – and in Derwentwater. The scientific name for the species

is *Coregonus albula* and it is a freshwater fish belonging to the Coregonidae or whitefishes. Seldom growing larger than 8 inches (20 cms) and with a distinctly pointed head the species is silvery blue or white on the flanks, greenish black on the back and has a white belly. Vendace are plankton feeders and are seldom caught by anglers and they may therefore be more common than is often suggested.

Not only are birdwatchers and anglers drawn to Bassenthwaite, but those with a literary bent also stand in pensive mood upon its banks at Mire House which is open at times during the summer season. Tennyson once stayed there and it has been suggested that he may have discussed the writing of *Morte d'Arthur* with his host, the well read James Spedding and possibly with other guests including Carlyle and Edward Fitzgerald. Was Bassenthwaite in the poet's mind when he wrote of the death of Arthur in *Idylls of the King* and did the grief stricken, but faithful Sir Bedevere hurl away Excalibur into the icy waters on that frosty night?

Another of Lakeland's unsung rivers, the Derwent, flows through both Derwentwater and Bassenthwaite on its way to join the Cocker at Cockermouth before reaching the sea at Workington which was once an important port. The river well deserves its name because Derwent is of Celtic origin and means clear water, an ideal description for this lovely river which is fished for sea and brown trout, salmon, perch and pike against a spectacular backdrop of glorious and varied landscapes. The land between Bassenthwaite and Derwentwater is obviously a flat flood plain and in the not too distant past the two lakes must have been united and their separation is a significant step towards the eventual silting up and disappearance of both shallow stretches of water. This on-going process was mentioned in chapter one and we wonder what future conservationists will want to do about this natural occurrence!

The land between Bassenthwaite and Derwentwater can be viewed from the churchyard of St Kentigern at Crossthwaite near Keswick. Here is buried the writer Robert Southey

*The moss land between Derwentwater and Bassenthwaite is excellent birdwatching country*

who, in his lifetime, was the most economically successful of the lake poets. The Victorian cleric Canon Rawnsley administered to the congregation here as well as finding time to be a co-founder of the National Trust. The canon was probably inspired by the splendid view from his churchyard.

Over the reedy areas of Bassenthwaite, predators hunt including hen harrier, merlin, kestrel, buzzard and sparrowhawk. Sedge, grasshopper, reed and willow warbler all breed as do reed bunting, dipper and common sandpiper. In the area of Bowness Bay we find the greatest concentrations of wildfowl due to a combination of factors including the activities of the sailing club which do not penetrate here and the fact that the area is sheltered. Up to 800 mallard and 500 teal occur regularly and scaup and long tailed duck both occur occasionally when heavy weather at sea drives them inland. Being shallow the lake has areas where vegetation pokes out above the water level and these make ideal perches for cormorants whilst herons also stalk patiently around in search of frogs and toads which breed in the shallows.

Above the lake and overlooking the River Derwent which flows out of Bassenthwaite and towards Derwentwater is Dodd's Wood with car park and associated nature trails which wind through sections of native deciduous and introduced coniferous areas with a variety of birds including woodcock, tawny owl, sparrowhawk, woodpigeon. All of these seem more common in winter whilst in summer spotted flycatcher, redstart, wood warbler and nightjar have all been recorded along with the usual species of thrush and warbler. Treecreepers roost in the larches and occasionally flocks of wintering siskins, long tailed tits and crossbills move through the area.

### Access

The A66 Keswick to Cockermouth road runs close alongside one bank of the lake with several parking places allowing good views over the water. Several car parks and view points are connected by a lakeside footpath from which excellent bird watching is possible. Access by car on the opposite side is not so easy the A591 Keswick to Carlisle road being much more elevated although footpaths do run through Dodd's Wood and around Bowness Bay. Set among trees is the ancient and attractive Pheasant Inn, which is residential and also provides a selection of excellent bar snacks.

*Chapter Six*

# *Thirlmere*

Prior to 1884 a tiny lake surrounded by a cluster of farms and cottages slept peacefully in a hollow of the lakeland hills. But the growing city of Manchester was thirsty and by 1894 Thirlmere reservoir had been built, stretched four miles in length, was half a mile wide, and from the dammed valley a 90 mile long pipeline carried Lakeland water to the city. The locals were not pleased and the water authority were, until recent years, decidedly hostile. Thirlmere despite bearing the imprint of human exploitation is a beautiful spot fringed by trees, both deciduous and coniferous, and its mellowing grandeur is criss-crossed by footpaths.

The wildlife accepted the change in the environment more quickly than many local folk and agile red squirrels and mighty red deer find welcome refuge here as do the occasional flocks of crossbills whilst sparrowhawks are increasingly common residents. Blue and great tits, as well as spotted and pied flycatchers use the nest boxes which have been provided in Thirlmere forest since 1912 and the authorities have also fed the birds in winter. Canada geese breed around the reservoir and can be seen through the trees from the Swirls Forest Nature Trail. A path now leads over the aqueduct and down across a number of lovely becks to the Kings

*Stags horn fungus grows well on the larch trees which surround Thirlmere*

Head Inn at Thirlspot, from which other paths lead up to Helvellyn.

At the head of Thirlmere stands the forlorn looking white church of Wythburn which survived the flooding of the valley, but this meant little since the rising waters had swallowed the homes and farms of its congregation. The only gathering here now is of the cars of those parked off the A591 and who are engaged in the easy climb of Helvellyn. An unusual sign off the road indicates Armboth a hamlet swallowed when the lake level was raised and all that remains of the garden of the once grand old hall is the monkey puzzle tree standing stark on the shore of the lake.

Over the next decade plans are afoot to replace the alien conifers with native deciduous trees and naturalists will doubtless be hoping that this is a continuing trend in our lakeland hills and valleys.

**Access**

The A591 runs alongside Thirlmere and the Forestry Commission's relaxation in attitudes to public access is demonstrated in the well organised trails and informative leaflets.

# Chapter Seven

# *Haweswater*

Manchester was still thirsty even after Thirlmere, and looked greedily towards the hamlet of Mardale which it knew well because much of its dairy produce came from the valley along an established railway link. What was it to be 3,000 pounds of butter per week or 18,660 million gallons of water? The authorities looked at tiny Haweswater and decided in the 1930s that the lake level could be raised by 95 feet (29 metres) and the valley dammed. Unfortunately this meant that the hamlet of Mardale with its lovely little church, rose garlanded cottages and the Dun Bull Inn had to be inundated. And so, despite protests, it came to pass and by 1940 Manchester was linked to Haweswater via a 9 mile tunnelled pipe line through Mardale, along the Longsleddale valley to Garnett Bridge near Kendal. From this point the waters of Haweswater and Thirlmere journey together to the city taps. The planners may have been insensitive during the construction of Thirlmere, but they had listened to criticism and this is reflected in a more sympathetic approach to landscaping when it came the turn of Hawswater. There are some panoramic views of the lake through the conifers especially beyond the Haweswater hotel, the only domestic building in the Dale and which has continued the licence

*The golden eagle breeds around Haweswater and attracts many visitors to the area*

once held by the Dun Bull.

Naturalists travel regularly to Haweswater these days and are not now repelled by the Water Company who have provided a car park from which the well publicised golden eagles may be watched soaring on the thermals high over Wallow Crag. Historians can also find food for thought in the valley in which Hugh Holme sought refuge in the 13th century after being implicated in a plot to kill King John and as a result was given the title King of Mardale. The cave in which he is said to have lived is in the still remote area of Riggindale. Close to the foot of the present lake is Thornthwaite Hall – the name thwaite being Norse for a woodland clearing – obviously relating to the period before the water level was raised and the site surrounded by woodlands. The Elizabethan building was the home of the Curwen family, but it has some literary connection with Anthony Trollope (1815-1882) and may well have been the setting for the first of his Palliser novels entitled *Can You Forgive Her?* published in 1864. It has to be admitted that at times Haweswater looks as natural as any other of the lakes especially on a tranquil winter's dawn when the snow-capped Harter Fell is mirrored in its surface.

## Access

From the A6 road at Shap turn left along a minor road towards Shap Abbey and Bampton. A minor cul-de-sac road from Bampton leads past Thornthwaite Hall, Burnbanks, a Mountain Rescue Post and Mardale Common to the head of the reservoir. A network of footpaths are sited around the reservoir leading off from the car park.

*Chapter Eight*

# Derwentwater

This shallow lake has long been famed as a skater's paradise and photographers are often seen queueing to take their place to capture a well known beauty spot. It receives its water from the River Derwent and from numerous streams which pour down in milky torrents from upland tarns. The most famous of these is Watendlath which drains down via the truly magnificent falls of Lodore. Screened by trees the 150 feet (46 metres) drop between Gowder and Shepherd's Crag can be something of a disappointment if visited in dry weather but following a deluge the power and awesome force of swirling, bucking and tormented water is violent enough to take the breath away.

Beautiful and equally haunting in any weather is the tiny hamlet of Watendlath itself, its farms clustered around a hump-backed bridge close to the tarn. Here Hugh Walpole (1884-1941) the New Zealander who wrote Lakeland novels better than the natives set his plot for *Judith Paris* which was published in 1931. Below the tarn and overlooking Derwentwater at Ashness is the packhorse bridge, probably photographed and drawn more than any other in Lakeland. It is impossible to look at the simplicity of its form or to sit and picnic near the stream and feed the birds

*A welcome rest for horse and rider in the cooling waters of Watendlath Tarn which is the setting for Walpole's novel "Judith Paris"*

Martineau thought "obtained more celebrity than it deserved". The sightings are usually in the late summer months and it is probably due to aquatic vegetation rotting and the gases so produced give the mass its buoyancy. It is interesting to note that this explanation has also occasionally been given to account for the Loch Ness Monster.

Derwentwater, however, has four real islands full of history and offering such magnificent views that it has no need of imaginary islands. These can be reached by boat or seen from the footpaths which follow the banks and meander through rich woodlands making Derwentwater the most attractive lake for walkers of all ages and physical abilities. Boat tours can be undertaken throughout the season, but sailing has never been easy here due to unpredictable cross winds howling down from the surrounding fells, but these have the compensation of making Derwentwater scenically dramatic. Each of the four islands, St Herbert's in the centre of the lake, Derwent Isle off Friar's Crag and Lord Island just to the south of Friar's Crag and Rampsholme Island all have their special charm but it is the first island which has the longest documented history. This was the retreat of St Herbert, a great friend of St

especially gulls and jackdaws without wanting to try just one more sketch or photograph despite the presence of others doing the same. Quite close to the falls of Lodore and a little to the north of the point where Watendlath Beck enters Derwentwater one of Lakeland's greatest mysteries can occasionally be witnessed. This is the so called 'floating island' which Harriet

Cuthbert, and Friar's Crag marks the spot where monks from Lindisfarne and other pilgrims waited for the ferry to take them over to the Shrine. Friar's Crag was listed by John Ruskin as one of Europe's top three viewpoints and this is underlined by the erosion caused by the footprints of tourists. Others would argue that the view from Castle Head is even better and from here the serene beauty of the lake shines out like a beacon and we can rejoice that so much is in the hands of the National Trust. Grange Fell was bought by H.R.H. the Princess Louise in memory of her brother King Edward VII whilst the awesome but impressive Scafell Pike was donated to the Trust in memory of Lakelanders who died in the First World War. They can have no finer memorial than this.

Derwentwater is a perfect centre for those who enjoy tramping the mountains as the attractive tourist town of Keswick snuggles close to its banks and beyond is the massive bulk of Skiddaw. This area has not always been peaceful and was once a bustling industrial centre for mining and the pencil factory at Greta Bridge reminds us of the once extensive plumbago which was mined in Borrowdale. This form of carbon is often called graphite and

Ashness Bridge, Derwentwater looking toward Keswick

*Ashness Bridge, Derwentwater looking toward Keswick*

59

this is the 'lead' used in pencils. These workings have gone the way of the copper mines which in the time of Elizabeth I were worked by Germans, but imported 'lead' is now used and the pencils are still a thriving industry set in one of the most idyllic spots in England. Keswick's most ancient building is the Church of St Kentigern at Crossthwaite parts of which date back to the 12th century, although most of the structure was built between the 14th and 16th

*Derwentwater looks at its best on early winter mornings with cloud rolling off the snow-capped mountains*

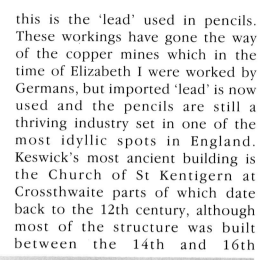

centuries. Greta Hall was once the home of two of Britain's most illustrious poets. Samuel Taylor Coleridge (1774-1834) lived here for a short period but Robert Southey lived here from 1803 until his death in 1843. Wordsworth is perhaps rightly regarded as the most formidable of the Lakeland's poets, but Southey at his best is one of the finest advocates of the beauty of the region.

Because it is so shallow Derwentwater has always been a popular spot for wildfowl and species such as coot, moorhen, grebe and warbler which find the reed fringed bays ideal for both roosting and breeding. During the height of the tourist season the walkers tend to drive the birds out into the centre of the lake or in the case of passerines up onto the narrow tree lined valleys or onto the wooded islands. In winter, however, when the cold tranquillity is only disturbed by the odd hardy fisherman the birds have the lake to themselves. Cormorants can reach a peak of around 40 during mid winter. All three of our naturally occurring swans are found here as is an increasing number of Canada geese. Flocks of up to 100 pochard, wigeon, teal and tufted duck are commonplace with several hundred mallard building up to a mid winter peak. Smaller counts of goldeneye, goosander, red breasted merganser, shelduck and even a scaup and long tailed duck have been recorded. During autumn there is a substantial gathering of passerines particularly swallows and martins on their way south and using the reed and iris beds as a roosting site whilst hawking for food over the water. At the same time flocks of fieldfare, redwing, blackbird and mistle thrush arrive from their northern breeding grounds and make short work of the rowan and hawthorn berries. Their presence often attracts birds of prey particularly the peregrine but also the occasional hen harrier and merlin. Buzzards have also become increasingly common in the area after a low point following a decline following the demise of the rabbit due to the myxamatosis outbreak of the 1950s. As the rabbit population has increased so the buzzard counts have risen although some birds still feed mainly on moles which they learned to exploit when rabbits were scarce.

High up above the lake and beyond Ashness Bridge is Watendlath Tarn which also has good counts of wildfowl including an increasing flock of Canada geese except in extreme weather when it tends to freeze over. Waders such as redshank, dunlin, common sandpiper and the occasional ruff and greenshank occur here. Soon after leaving the tarn a swift-moving stream tumbles over the falls of Lodore. Below the falls the swift stream is an ideal habitat for dipper and grey wagtail whilst in the damp woodlands fringing the water the insect population is high enough to support both spotted and pied flycatchers as well as redstart and both green and great spotted woodpeckers. Close to Lodore, but on the main lake, in December 1980 the Cumbrian Bird report notes the sighting of a juvenile black necked grebe.

**Access**
Easily reached from the M6 via the A66 Keswick stands on the banks of Derwentwater and from the car parks in town and strewn along the banks of the lake (followed by the B5289) a network of footpaths lead into the woodland and lakeside walks. Most are under the control of the National Trust and are freely accessible. Despite its popularity with tourists the area has many quiet spots which abound with birds and the associated life forms upon which they rely.

# Chapter Nine

# *Crummock Water*

Many of the English lakes derive their names from the Scandinavian language but Crummock is truly Anglo-Saxon and means crooked which is a perfect description for the whole of the valley which also includes Buttermere. Indeed Buttermere village lies between its own lake and Crummock Water. The two lakes have doubtless been connected at one time and because they are so close together it is inevitable that folk compare them, usually to the detriment of Crummock. This is hardly fair since both have their own unique charm. We well remember one memorable summers walk around Crummock when a cuckoo called continuously from an outcrop, a buzzard soared high over the blue of the lake and energetic lambs jumped round in the lush greenery of the meadows. In his own isolated field of heifers a grand old Hereford bull slept away the heat of day swatting flies with the occasional whip of his tail.

The National Trust own a sizeable chunk of the bank and a few rowing boats are available for hire and enable the 3 miles length to be explored at leisure. On one special day we watched a heron catch an eel, a kingfisher flash across an inlet and a bitch otter with her cub feeding on a fine looking perch. Having a maximum depth of 144 feet (43.9 metres) the water is cool

*Foxhounds on the banks of Crummock Water about 1930*

enough for char to be at home and there are also some good specimens of pike and brown trout. Walks leading up to Rannerdale Knot and along Gale Fell to the 120 feet (36.5 metres) drop of Scale Force are well worth the effort. The views of Whiteless Pike reflected in Crummock's surface are often breathtaking in their clarity and variety of colour. Langthwaite Wood is a mass of springtime blossom, summer birds, autumn fungi and provides a wintertime shelter for those who appreciate the beauty of Crummock, an underrated water at all times and in all weathers.

Crummock Water carries a varied, but never substantial population of wildfowl because its depth of 144 feet (43.9 metres) tends to make it a little cool and lacking in nutrients. Its neighbour Buttermere, however, is much shallower having a maximum depth of only 94 feet (31.02 metres) (see page 76) This accounts for its winter popularity with wildfowl when as many as 30 whooper swans may be seen together with up to 300 mallard and pochard, with slightly fewer tufted duck. Teal, goldeneye, goosander and red breasted merganser are all regularly recorded as are the occasional shelduck, pintail, shoveler and long tailed duck. During spring there is a regular passage of waders including dunlin and common sandpiper whilst during April and May common and black tern have been spotted.

## Access

Both lakes are best explored on foot using as a base Buttermere which is conveniently sited between the two and having a fair amount of parking space close to the Fish Hotel. Buttermere is also served by the Mountain Goat mini-bus service from Keswick which runs four times daily with connections for Ullswater, Windermere and Ambleside. There are well signed footpaths to both lakes and to the splendid Scale Force waterfall which tumbles some 100 feet (30.5 metres) between jagged rocks. The footpaths provide excellent bird watching viewpoints and sheltered picnic spots, but the tree fringed reedy bays of Buttermere are best watched from the lake itself. Rowing boats can be hired from the nearby Gatesgarth farm and I know several birdwatchers who find the boats are ideal mobile hides which, providing the watchers keep still, are ignored by the birds. The lakes are overlooked by the B5289 which leaves Keswick alongside Derwentwater, swings around Seatoller and over Buttermere Fell towards the two lakes and thence to Cockermouth.

*Chapter Ten*

# Wastwater

Wastwater is reached by turning off the A595 road at Gosforth where a stop should be made to look at the old cross which dominates the churchyard. Many walkers use the miniature railway known locally as *Lile Ratty* which carries summer passengers high into Eskdale passing Muncaster mill which has been restored and produces excellent wholemeal flour. The single track railroad was originally built to carry quarried stone to the main railhead at Ravenglass. Wasdale is rightly the Mecca for Lakeland worshippers whether they seek the mighty Lingmell, Kirk Fell, Yewbarrow or the gaunt bulk of Great Gable. Behind Lingmell, Scafell and Scafell Pike can be seen and are within reach of the energetic. It is small wonder that the area is the climbing centre of Lakeland and many a tale is told over the bar of the Wastwater Hotel but few stories will be taller than those credited to its celebrated landlord Will Ritson. He was a contemporary of Wordsworth, had an impish sense of humour and was said to be the biggest liar in England. Above the hotel is Ritson Falls thus perpetuating the man who lived to the ripe old age of 83 before passing away in the tiny hamlet of Strands, sited on the River Irt which runs out of the western foot of the lake. In November 1989 we joined the

*The Gosforth Cross, one of the most important religious artefacts in Britain*

crowds at the Bridge Inn at Santon Bridge overlooking the River Irt to celebrate Will Ritson's life of happy fibbing. As we ate our 'tatie pie' supper we listened to John Reeves win the title of the Biggest Liar in the World a competition started in 1975 and ensures that Will Ritson's name will live forever in Cumbrian folklore. Perhaps his laughter still rings out over the surface of his beloved Wastwater.

Wastwater is one of Lakeland's clearest lakes and is described as oligotrophic which is the scientists' way of explaining that it is so deep and cold that few organisms can live in it. Shallower warmer lakes such as Esthwaite tend to be full of organisms, a condition known as eutrophic. Such lakes tend to lack clarity. There is, however, enough food in Wastwater to feed brown trout and char which both occur here, the latter finding conditions ideal. This is because at 260 feet (almost 75 metres) it is the deepest stretch of water in the Lake District and is 3 miles (4.8 km) long and 0.5 mile (o.8 km) across. The lake is overlooked by a fantastic sweep of scree which comes right down to the water's edge, and which is so unstable that it often shutters down into the lake. The area around the lake is owned by the National Trust

*Wastwater on a misty autumn morning*

and the real wonder of Wastwater is best seen by walking through the woods to the south of the Youth Hostel which echo with spring bird song and is bursting with colourful flowers. At the dawn of a winter's day following overnight snow there is no finer sight in the world as the pink flush touches the summit of the hills and warns of more snow to come. The local rhyme of 'red in the morning, shepherds' warning' is often proved true. The remote silence of Wastwater seems likely to continue as motor boats are not allowed and only a few sailing boats are launched from the rocky shore. The only threat is posed by the proposal by the North West Water Authority who want to extract water from Wastwater and Ennerdale and pipe it to the nuclear power complex at Windscale and to other consumers in West Cumbria.

**Access**

One of the most remote spots in Lakeland, much of the area is administered by the National Trust. There are a few parking areas, but most visitors come in on foot. Wastwater is best approached via the A595 Millom to Carlisle road and turning off at Gosforth and thence to Wasdale and the lake. Some folk arrive in the area by travelling on the single track *Ratty* railway from Ravenglass and then by foot into one of the finest climbing areas in the country. Those who are prepared to work hard physically for their birds are occasionally rewarded by sightings of dotterel, snow bunting, golden plover and golden eagle which also enjoy the solitude of the high tops.

# Chapter Eleven

# Ennerdale

With a depth of 148 feet (45 metres) Ennerdale does not contain a great deal of food for birds but the Forestry Commission's new plantations combined with some natural deciduous woodland has proved attractive. Both black and red grouse are seen as are short eared owls and the strikingly white barn owl with its mottled brown back. Birds of prey include buzzard which soar over the surrounding crags around Great Gable and sparrowhawk which hunt along the corridors between lake and woodland. Here also is the lake which Wordsworth described as the 'haunt of Cormorant and the Sea Mews clang' and the scent of rose and honeysuckle diffuses into the air already vibrating to the sound of lark and curlew, whilst from the larches below Bowness Knott the picnicker with a sharp ear can hear the sound of the tiny goldcrests.

It is hard to imagine a more attractive site for a lake and from the western shore of Ennerdale the view towards Steeple and Pillar mountains is one of Lakeland's gems. Bowness Knott and Anglers' Crag watch over the lake, which is circled by a tangle of footpaths and few buildings disturb the traditional tranquility of the scene. Even the water extracted for the ratepayers of the Whitehaven area has disturbed not a single ripple. The Water

*A farmer carting bracken from the slopes around Ennerdale. In the 1930s bracken was used as bedding for animals and was burned to produce fertiliser*

Authority's request for a larger extraction from the lake is, however, being sensibly resisted. The River Liza enters one end of the lake which absorbs it completely the river emerging from the opposite end being the Ehen which chuckles its merry way through a surprisingly attractive man-made weir to Ennerdale Bridge.

**Access**

Although Ennerdale is difficult to reach by road the National Trust have provided a car park by the lake at the end of a rough track. From Cockermouth follow the A5086 towards Frizington and Egremont. From this a minor road leads via Kirkland, Crossdale and the Anglers' Inn to Ennerdale car park.

# Chapter Twelve

# *Esthwaite*

*"My morning walks*
*Were early; oft before the hours of*
*school*
*I travelled round our little lake*
*Of pleasant wanderings. Happy*
*time."*

So wrote Wordsworth of his schooldays, and we were lucky enough to spend our youth around the same spot and what a good training for country lovers it is. Esthwaite is a highly evolved and nutrient rich lake which scientists called eutrophic. It is only 80 feet (24.3 metres) at its deepest point and is fringed by reeds in the shallow marshy areas. Priests' Pot at the head of the lake has already been separated from the main lake due to centuries of silting and has been set up as a National Nature Reserve in order to study how fens develop from shallow lakes. Priests' Pot refers to the fact that it was once used by the monks of Furness Abbey as a fish farm although those with a lower opinion of the brethren said that the pot held as much as a thirsty monk could drink in good old English ale. There are some excellent access points around the shores of Esthwaite but most of the bank and all of the lake is owned by the Sandys family and their 16th century hall is close to the south west shore, but they now prefer to live at nearby Graythwaite Hall.

One of the family, Archbishop

*Bullrushes or more accurately described as reed-mace growing in profusion around Esthwaite*

Sandys endowed the Grammar School which Wordsworth attended at nearby Hawkshead which was once the commercial and industrial hub of the district. It was an important wool town way back in Norman times and at one time it had seven busy inns to cope with visitors which arrived by coach. Hawkshead was owned by the monks of Furness for upwards of 400 years and its narrow twisting cobbled streets overlooked by spinning galleries made driving through it in later centuries a hazardous enterprise. In 1974 the village was by-passed and an attractive and spacious car park provided. Visitors may now stroll around in peace and concentrate on the Grammar School and Ann Tyson's cottage where the boy Wordsworth lodged.

Signed from Hawkshead is Grizedale Forest with its Visitors' Centre, Theatre, spacious car park and nature trails all of which combine to produce one of the most attractive and popular tourist areas in Lakeland. There are hides from which red and roe deer can be observed but the nature trails feature wooden sculptures created by visiting artists. At first we thought that these may have been an intrusion and interfere with those studying the wildlife, but we were wrong and now look forward to

*A coach and four passes through Hawkshead and provides a reminder of the good old days*

*One of the wooden
sculptures at
Grizedale Forest*

sharing the humour of the sculptures with those who created these semi-natural masterpieces. The damp areas of the woodlands are the haunt of adder and common lizard.

To follow the poet's route to Esthwaite is still one of our joys whatever the season or weather conditions. Its banks echo to the sound of wintering wildfowl, shine with springtime and summer flowers, whilst the red berries of autumn rowan, rose and hawthorn reflected in the tranquil shallows of the reed fringed Esthwaite are breathtakingly beautiful.

Esthwaite is also a favourite with wildfowl with up to 150 tufted duck being present in August and almost 300 goldeneye being recorded in January. Barnacle geese turn up occasionally and are probably storm tossed birds from the wintering flocks on the Scottish bank of the Solway. An increasing flock of pink footed geese are also a feature of Esthwaite as are small numbers of whooper and Bewick swans. Coot also use the sheltered bays as a winter refuge and as many as 150 are often counted and the cormorant roost occasionally numbers 50 birds.

**Access**

There are excellent car parks dotted along the shore which is followed

74

*The adder is quite common in the damp areas around Esthwaite*

by the B5289 leading from Hawkshead to the Windermere Ferry via Far Sawrey. The best bird watching areas are on the western shore just off the minor road from Hawkshead to Newby Bridge.

*Chapter Thirteen*

# *Buttermere*

As we have seen the hamlet of Buttermere is shared by Crummock Water and its own lake. The tiny modern church of St James, perched high on a rocky knoll is charming and blessed with some magnificent woodwork and a ceiling with 16 benevolent looking angels smiling down at the worshippers. For almost 700 years Buttermere, along with Cockermouth, Embleton, Wythop and Lorton was part of the immense parish of Brigham and the provision of an ordained priest for each hamlet was thought an unnecessary expense and they were served by unordained readers. One such was 'Wonderful Walker' who died in 1803 in his 93rd year and despite the low stipends paid to readers left the princely sum of £2000. This says much for the man's industry and he not only wrote letters for the illiterate, ploughed fields for the lazy, was prepared to spin cloth for the sick, but also made good use of clog-shoes, harden sark, whittle-gate and goose-gate. These were customs to ensure that the Reader had shoes, clothes, food and board and the right to allow his goose free grazing on the common. No wonder Wonderful Walker lived long and died rich.

Buttermere was one of the favourite spots of Victorian visitors to

Lakeland in pursuit of the story first described by Coleridge, Southey and Wordsworth not to mention a host of melodramas acted out on the London stage. The sad saga took place in 1802 when Mary Robinson, the 18 year old daughter of the landlord of the Fish Inn, came face to face with 'the evil of the city'. Known as the Beauty of Buttermere, Mary was seduced and bigamously married by John Hatfield posing as the 'Hon. Col. Hope'. He was eventually hanged at Carlisle for forgery, and it is good to relate that Mary's second marriage was happier and she lived to a ripe old age almost unaware of the fame thrust upon her by the writings of the Lakeland poets and the London dramatists.

Buttermere still attracts many holiday coaches and is served by a

*The Fish Hotel – the home of Mary, the Beauty of Buttermere*

mini-bus service from Keswick, and which is well named the Mountain Goat. It runs four times daily and there are connections to Ullswater, Windermere and Ambleside. From the car parks near the Fish Inn paths lead around the lake overlooked by the towering bulk of High Style, High Crag and Red Pike down which tumbles the frothing waters of the well named Sour Milk Gill. We once saw a kingfisher flash through the fringing trees and along the lake edge on which over 30 whooper

*St James' Church at Buttermere*

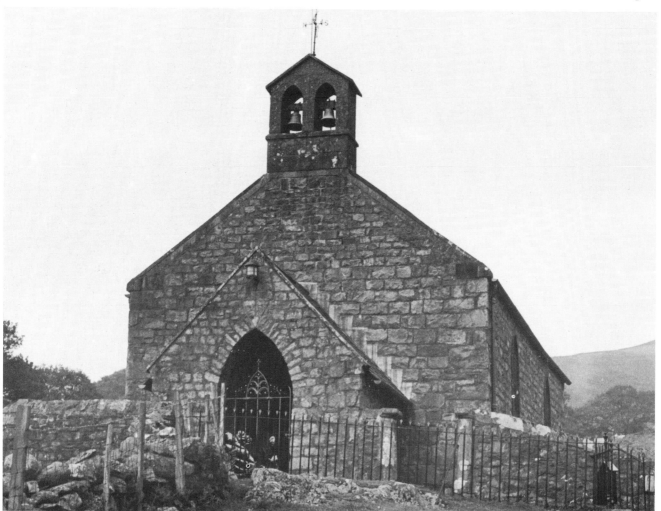

*Buttermere*

*Buttermere*

swans were wintering along with several hundred pochard, the red heads of the drakes reflecting in the early morning sunshine. Much of the area is in the hands of the National Trust including the often muddy walk to Scale Force one of the finest waterfalls in Lakeland tumbling down over 100 feet (30.5 metres) between jagged rocks. Those wishing to explore Buttermere's wooded bays can hire a rowing boat from Gatesgarth Farm, and will find themselves following the athletic example of the Lakes Poets who wrote so eloquently about the Beauty of Buttermere.

**Access**

Buttermere is best explored along with its larger companion, Crummock Water, described on page 62.

# Chapter Fourteen

# Loweswater

Loweswater has the unusual feature of its water draining out via Park Beck and twisting inwards towards the central valley and into Crummock Water to which it was undoubtedly joined prior to the ice melting. Like most of the lakes it is best appreciated from the water surface itself and there are rowing boats for hire. The National Trust woodlands, which clothe the banks, are popular with birds including the green woodpecker which is expanding its range in Lakeland. We were once lucky enough to see an osprey perched on an old birch tree, tearing away at a fish which it had caught in the lake. A lovely panoramic view of Loweswater can be had from the summit of the 1643 feet (511 metres) Mellbreak Hill, but walkers are advised to stick to the marked route and wear good stout footwear. The air on the hill is as fresh as any in Lakeland and it seems to have been good for the local clergy. John Borranskail was buried in Loweswater church in the year 1674 after serving as a cleric for 73 years and Thomas Cowper arrived in 1744 and served until 1795!

The lake lovers should also direct their attention to the southern end of Loweswater, which has a decidedly more pastoral air about it than its neighbours Crummock and Buttermere, and a stroll through Holme Wood which winds up the

*Loweswater is a lake for all seasons and provides excellent birdwatching from the shelter of fringing trees*

slope of Carling Knott is magnificent. From the trees the cattle can often be seen wading in the reedy shallows which fringe a lake which has a maximum depth of 60 feet (18.3 metres). Seldom is the lonely quiet of Loweswater disturbed, but it is the focus of the dales' folks attention on show day held in September when hound trailing which is the local sport – some would say religion – takes over the hills and dales. Trailing is a drag hunt prior to which a walker drags a soaked rag of aniseed over a circular and well plotted course, and the wonderfully fit and finely trained hounds chase the scent. Whistles blow, locals and visitors cheer, children scream, hounds bay, losers despair, winners grin and bookmakers drive their big cars back to the towns. In a day or two the wind blows away the litter, the wildfowl call gently in the reeds and the cows crop away at the rich green grass by the side of the lake.

The sheltered reed fringed shallows are ideal for waterbirds including grebe and wildfowl amongst which are red breasted merganser, goosander, goldeneye (often in flocks of up to 50) pochard, mallard, teal and wigeon. The latter roost on the water but feed on the lush green fields surrounding the lake. They are often accompanied, especially between November and February, by flocks of golden plover and lapwings with the occasional group of ruff whilst in the damper areas snipe are frequent visitors along with redshank and curlew. In spring both green and common sandpiper are recorded and a few pairs of the latter remain to breed before returning south in the autumn.

**Access**

From Cockermouth either the A5089 or B5292 if followed south will lead to Loweswater which is well signed. There is limited parking although there is usually no problem out of the high season. Birdwatchers should certainly have no problem during the winter.

# Chapter Fifteen

# *Grasmere*

*Coniston fox hounds with Grasmere in the background (about 1920)*

'Grassy Grasmere and Reedy Rydal' are affectionate terms for a brace of Lakeland's most attractive stretches of water, separated only by a marshy area which clearly reveals that the two were once part of the same lake. William Wordsworth loved them both and in her journal, which was never intended for publication, his sister Dorothy describes the larger of the two as "our dear Grasmere." There are two suggested explanations of the name and the grassy mere would seem to fit since it is indeed reed fringed but the generally accepted view is that it derives from the Norse Gris-Mere meaning the mere-of-the-pigs. Doubtless the wild boar did roam

free in the woods around the lake which is 1 mile (1.6 kms) long by 0.5 mile (0.8 km) wide and has a maximum depth of 75 feet (22.8 metres). The lake is therefore sufficiently eutrophic to support good fishing and Dorothy Wordsworth's journal mentions the landing of a 7 pound pike. Wildfowl are present throughout the year with several pairs of tufted duck, mallard and teal breeding around the reedy edges, their numbers swelled in winter when they are joined by other species particularly pochard, goosander and swans. Great crested grebe are also present throughout the year, and the walk along the footpath through the National Trust woodlands are home to an amazing variety of small birds. Apart from the obvious attractions of treading the same paths as literary giants such as Coleridge, Southey, De Quincey, Sir Walter Scott and of course Wordsworth, Grasmere has other gems to offer the tourist. The annual Rushbearing and the Sports are two of Lakeland's most popular attractions.

*Grasmere and Rydal Lakes*

*Grasmere,
Wordsworth's parish
church*

*Rushbearing near Grasmere in the 1930s*

One of our earliest memories is of being taken by an ancient charabanc to see the Rushbearing which takes place on the nearest Saturday to St Oswald's day which is on the 5th August, and to whom the church is dedicated. It was so hot that the tar on the road was melting, and clutching a dripping ice-cream in one hand and mother's arm with the other, we were hustled through the crowd to the churchyard. Brass bands played, children in their colourful new clothes marched purposefully with bundles of grass, red faced dancing troupes went through their paces, and dalesmen looked on with friendly eyes. It was too hot for them to wear jackets and there they stood, shirt sleeves rolled up and trousers supported by both belt and braces. Careful chaps were these Fells men! No amount of heat would ever persuade them to remove their caps, but they did yield a little to the weather and wear them at a rakish angle! Rushbearing is now a ceremony, but one which was obviously an adult task in the days when St Oswald's had only an earth floor and no form of heating. Rushes were gathered from the shore of the lake and carried in bundles to spread on the church floor and afterwards the church funds provided liberal quantities of ale! On that lovely August day we contented ourselves by queueing at a tiny cottage near to the lych gate of the church. Between 1660 and 1854 this was the school, but it now sells 'Sarah Nelson's Original Celebrated Grasmere Gingerbread'.

An equally exciting and even noisier day in Grasmere takes place on a well advertised Thursday towards the end of August when over 10,000 people gather to watch Grasmere sports. The grunts of wrestlers held tight together in true Cumberland and Westmorland style, mingle with the howling of hounds on the trail and the cheers for the fellrunners who race to the summit of Butter Crag and back. These sports may well date back to the days of the Vikings when trials of strength were but a training for war.

Don't forget to look for the Swan Hotel, to which Sir Walter Scott used to sneak for a 'wee dram' when staying with Wordsworth who kept a 'dry house'. Stand at the bridge near the village centre and watch the trout swimming beneath in the clear pools of the River Rothay. Pause a while in the 12th century church of St Oswald and read Wordsworth's description of it, published in 'The Excursion'.

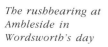

*The rushbearing at Ambleside in Wordsworth's day*

*"Not raised in nice proportions was
   the pile,
But large and massy; for duration
   built;
With pillars crowded, and the roof
   upheld
By naked rafters, intricately crossed,
Like leafless underboughs in some
   thick wood,
All withered by the depth of shade
   above. "*

Our final view of Grasmere,
however, should be of the lake itself
which is seen at its best from
Loughrigg Terrace, reached from
the south eastern side of the lake by
a well used path climbing about 200
feet (61 metres) above the bank
revealing the full splendour of the
Mere of the Wild Pigs in the
foreground with the rugged might
of Helm Crag as a spectacular
backcloth of ever- hanging colour as
clouds drive across its face.

### Access

The A591 road Kendal to Keswick
road runs alongside Rydal Water and
although Grasmere has now been by
passed the road into the village with
its spacious car park is well signed.
White Moss car park is also well
signed and easily seen from the
road. Well marked footpaths lead
into excellent bird watching
woodlands and it is only at the
height of the tourist season that
other visitors become numerous
enough to distract the serious
birdwatchers.

*Dove Cottage, on the
outskirts of
Grasmere, was once
the home of the
Wordsworth family*

# Chapter Sixteen

# Rydal Water

One of our personal favourites, Rydal Water is often described as the skaters' pond which is not surprising since at just under 60 feet (18 metres) at its deepest it does freeze easily. When Wordsworth lived at Rydal Mount it must have been a secluded spot, but between the house and the lake the A591 has been built and carries an often heavy stream of traffic between Keswick to Windermere. The southern side of the reed fringed lake has kept most of its old serenity despite the droves of people who, in summer, follow the path over the footbridge spanning the River Rothay in Rydal village and upwards through woodlands colourful with a stunning variety of flowers. It is at its best in May when it is carpeted with bluebells. If you want to see Rydal as Wordsworth would have recognised it pay a visit on a winter's morning and see how the lake is delightfully squeezed between the huge plateau of Loughrigg Fell to the south and the savage and rocky mass of Nab Scar to the north. This is excellent mammal country and bank vole, common shrew, fox and badger are all residents here abouts. The Wordsworths were not the only family of note to dwell within sight and sound of Rydal and its varied wildlife. The Fleming family resided at Rydal Hall for the best part of 400 years. Sir David Fleming was a

Church, King and Countryman to the last. He was a Royalist in the Civil War, was knighted for repressing Quakers after the Restoration and thought enough of his native county to compile an account of the Scandinavian influence upon it. His son became Bishop of Carlisle and Rydal Park now belongs to that Diocese, and is used as a conference and study centre although the fields are used for an important sheep dog trial in August.

Close to Rydal Hall is Wordsworth's Seat from which he could gaze in apprecition across to the lake and watch the winter wildfowl flight into land against the red orb of a setting sun. We can still do this but the headlights of cars on the A591 can sometimes be a little off putting. When he was living at Rydal Mount it is surprising how many now famous literary men lived close by or visited Wordsworth. De Quincey, self confessed opium eater, lived at Dove Cottage after Wordsworth and

*Rydal Water viewed from the footpath which runs around it*

*Bluebells grow in profusion around Rydal Water with the occasional white flower being found*

married the daughter of Farmer Simpson who lived at Nab Cottage which still stands with the date 1702 proudly carved over its door. Southey, Scott and Coleridge came here and William when out walking often called in at Fox How to chat with Dr Arnold of Rugby fame. He built the house and knew and loved the area well enough to humourously refer to the three possible roads from Rydal to Grasmere as Bit-by-Bit reform, Radical Reform and the best of all Old Corruption. Wordsworth's house, now restored to resemble the period when the poet lived there from 1813 to 1850 is owned by the National Trust and open to the public. For those who prefer the outdoor pursuit of perfection the National Trust also administer Whitemoss Common formerly a quarry but now a well appointed and spacious picnic site at the western end of Rydal Water. The old road to Grasmere is on the opposite side of the present A591 and from its summit there are spectacular views of the lake and it has the added advantage of passing by Wordsworth's old home at Dove Cottage. Rydal and its environs offer as wide a selection of wildlife as anywhere in Lakeland. Long tailed tits and siskins scuttle through the winter alders, water rails squeal

*The badger is very much at home in the woodlands around Rydal Water and Grasmere*

from the reeds, common sandpipers follow the path of the River Rothay from Grasmere and rest on the pebbly banks fringed with water forget-me-knot, kingcups and butterbur once used by the villages to wrap up their butter before the days of grease proofed paper. This delightful feeling of rustic domesticity set among dramatic scenery is still present round Rydal Water for those who have enough time to spare to recognise and savour it.

# Chapter Seventeen

# Brothers Water

The geometric shape of this 70 acre lake has led to two suggestions regarding its origins. The first is that it was built by the monks and the second is that it should be regarded as a tarn. There is no doubt, however, that it is naturally formed and that it was once part of Ullswater which became isolated as a result of silt being flushed down from the surrounding fells. This damp area became stabilised and Brothers Water is now two miles south of Ullswater at the foot of the awe inspiring Kirkstone pass close to the village of Hartsop. Nearby is Sykeside farm, the home until his death in 1936 at the age of 83 of one of Lakeland's most colourful characters. Charlie Dixon never moved away from his beloved lakes and yet rightly has a reputation of one of the world's finest landscape photographers. He must certainly have been inspired by the rugged beauty of Brothers Water its stony banks illuminated by flashes of yellow from kingcups and warmed by the red of ragged robin.

Close to the lake and commanding a panoramic view down the Dovedale valley is the historic Hartsop Hall, parts of which are 16th century, but the de Lancaster family made many tasteful alterations during the following century. Lord Lonsdale, of boxing's Lonsdale Belt fame, owned the hall at the end of the 17th century and local tradition insists that he built an extension which blocked the ancient footpath. Dalesmen always know their rights and once each year they trekked through the house to ensure their right of way was not allowed to lapse. Low Hartsop is a lovely hamlet, its surrounding fields sprinkled by the waters of Pasture Beck, and the whole scene giving an insight into what life was like in dear old Westmorland. There is the remains of an old water driven corn mill, a 16th century drying kiln and quaint cottages with open spinning galleries designed to provide maximum light in the days before electricity. Folk in those days lived by the sun, their only light being from rushes dipped in animal fat.

The village can become busy in the summer but is usually quiet and footpaths climb towards the soaring and often deserted hills in which nestles Hayes Water Tarn. Beyond it the lofty magnificence of High Street beckons the toughened walker. It is no wonder that Charlie Dixon found scenery for his camera near enough to his birthplace ever to consider moving away. His *Westmorland Shepherd* and *The Shepherd and the Lost Sheep* have captured for ever the rustic magnificence of a bygone age.

**Access**

The A592 road from Patterdale towards Kirkstone Pass passes close to Hartsop village and Brothers Water itself where cars can be parked. Well signed footpaths lead through Low Wood from Hartsop Hall and there are excellent viewpoints over the water.

*Chapter Eighteen*

# *Elterwater*

At Skelwith Bridge on the road between Coniston and Ambleside, a gently winding road leads to the smallest of the English lakes – Elterwater which is less than mile long and never deeper than 70 feet (21.3 metres). The early Scandinavian warriors who settled hereabouts called it Elpt Vatn which translates as the lake of the swans. Tradition states that the first wild swans to arrive in the Lake District each winter settle on the waters of Elpt Vatn before sampling the other lakes. Observations do not prove this, but it is good story nevertheless. In Britain we have the resident mute swan with its orange and black bill with the prominent knob at its base. In winter it is joined by the whooper and Bewick swans which breed far away in Scandinavia and Russia. The whooper is the same size as the mute swan being 5 feet 6 inches (150 cms) long and its bill is black and yellowish with the extensive yellow area ending in a point. The Bewick swan is much smaller and is never bigger than 4 feet (120 cms) and although it also has a black and yellow bill the yellow patch is much smaller and always ends bluntly. Remember B for Bewick and also for blunt. Elterwater itself is privately owned but the National Trust owns sufficient land on the north and eastern banks of the tree-lined lake to allow extensive

*A Whooper Swan on Elterwater, known for centuries as "Swan Lake"*

views over the water. The Langdale Pikes towering over the lake and village never seem anything but friendly even in the depths of winter.

Elterwater is fed by the mighty torrent of the Great Langdale Beck but the river as it emerges from the opposite end is renamed the Brathay. Looking down on the lake from the high road it is easy to see that it has been gradually silting up over the centuries due to sediment carried by the Great Langdale Beck. It was once much larger and deeper and the reed beds which are so attractive to the birds are also playing their part in destroying the lake. It will take many more centuries but eventually –if left to nature – Elterwater will be no more

and instead we shall have first a swamp and then a wooded valley.

The village of Elterwater has also changed its character. Gone is the gunpowder mill which was powered by Great Langdale Beck. The village green, however remains, its centre dominated by a spreading sycamore surrounded by seats. Maple Tree Corner is appropriately on one side whilst Beech Tree Corner is at the other. The Britannia Inn serves ale to walkers throughout the afternoon and many drink and eat outside in the beer garden even in the depths of winter. Walkers are a hardy lot! The telephone kiosk is painted grey and blends perfectly with the environment and the car parking and toilet facilities are both efficient and discreet.

Although a caravan site now occupies the site of the gunpowder works there is still some quarrying for hard slate and we have heard some visitors to the National Park complaining at the presence of industry. As born and bred Lakelanders we take exception to this as the area has always been industrialised and jobs are still important. We should also remember that it is not the cars of the summer visitors, nor the explosive echoes of the quarry which are the essence of Elterwater but the majesty of the wintering swans which have been visiting this delightful little lake since before recorded time.

## Access

Elterwater is privately owned but the National Trust have sufficient land on the north and eastern banks of the tree-lined lake to allow extensive views over the lake from the footpath. The Langdale Pikes tower over the lake and village. Elterwater village is reached by turning off the A593 Ambleside to Coniston road at Skelwith Bridge. Then follow the B5343 road to Elterwater where there is a substantial car park.

*A path running around Elterwater provides a wonderful winter's walk*

# Chapter Nineteen

# Tarn Hows

Few Lakeland scenes have been more photographed than Tarn Hows which is sometimes quoted as an example of the unspoiled beauty of the area. Visitors pour out of the spacious National Trust car parks to stand on the grassy knolls overlooking the stretch of water in which are mirrored the fringe of trees especially the red trunked Scots pines and graceful birches. Under the birches the red and white fly agaric fungus grows prolifically in the autumn. As they picnic against a magnificent backdrop of the Langdale Pikes and beyond these towards Red Screes and Helvellyn comments are made about unspoiled beauty. It comes as something of a shock to learn that Tarn Hows is, in fact, man-made. It is known that in 1598 there was a cottage called Tarnhouse around which were three small areas of still water. Tarn comes from the Norse and means 'a tear drop', a term which tells us that not all members of this fierce race were lacking in sentiment or a feeling for the finer things in life. In 1863 an ingenious system of dams joined the three into single tarn and we must admit that for once man had improved on nature. This should not, however, persuade us to try to repeat the experiment elsewhere in Lakeland. On a memorable January day we strolled among the carefully planned

*One man and his dog on ice at Tarn Hows*

nature trails laid out by the National Trust and Lake District Naturalists' Trust. Skaters enjoyed themselves on the ice and a walker persuaded his dog to take a short cut across the unfamiliar surface. Waterfalls had frozen during the night and icicles were hanging from every rock and shining in the afternoon sun. It became warm during the early afternoon and we saw both a buzzard and a raven soaring on the currents of air rising from the land. Long tailed tits and siskin fed on the alders, which were already developing catkins. Later in the year the long tailed tits breed in the area, with their bottle-shaped nest being

*Tarn Hows, overlooked by birch trees, is man-made but now looks as natural as any stretch of water in the Lake District*

one of the most beautifully designed as any species in the world.

The shallow water has a varied, if not spectacular variety of wildfowl and the reedy areas are popular with coot, moorhen, great crested grebe and the occasional water rail. Waterfalls plunge down into the sloping woodland and below these

dipper, grey wagtail and common sandpiper all breed. The presence of conifers has encouraged wood ants and their nests attract green woodpecker and jay. Red squirrels are resident in the Scots pines whilst in winter tree creepers roost in crevices in their red trunks and passing flocks of crossbills are sometimes encouraged to overwinter. Sparrowhawk, tawny, long eared and the occasional little owl have also been noted as have been nightjar, red grouse and woodcock. Peregrine, merlin and short eared owl are all seen occasionally on the fellside probably in search of breeding wheatear, meadow pipit and skylark.

**Access**

The car park above Tarn Hows is reached via a narrow one-way system of roads signed off the A593 Ambleside to Coniston road.

You can never be a naturalist without being an optimist and any black moods which do develop can soon be dispelled by a visit to any one of Cumbria's beautiful natural lakes – and then there is always the man-made Tarn Hows as a bonus!

*The Buzzard*
*– one of Lakeland's*
*most spectacular birds*
*of prey.*

*Illustration courtesy of*
*Carole Pugh*

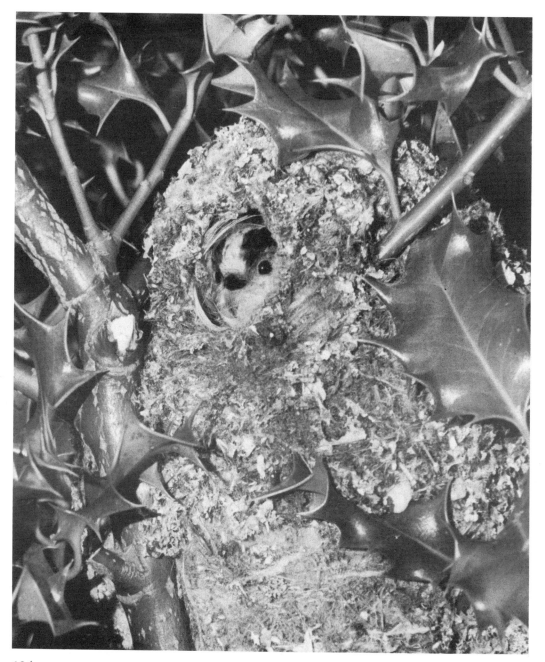

# NORTHERN CLASSIC REPRINTS

## The Manchester Man
### (Mrs. G. Linnaeus Banks)
Re-printed from an 1896 illustrated edition — undoubtedly the finest limp-bound edition ever. Fascinating reading, includes Peterloo. Over 400 pages, wonderfully illustrated.

ISBN 1 872226 16 7 £4.95

## The Manchester Rebels
### (W Harrison Ainsworth)
A heady mixture of fact and fiction combined in a compelling story of the Jacobean fight for the throne of England. Manchester's involvement and the formation of the Manchester Regiment. Authentic illustrations.

ISBN 1 872226 29 9 £4.95

## Hobson's Choice (the Novel)
### (Harold Brighouse)
The humorous and classic moving story of Salford's favourite tale. Well worth re-discovering this enjoyable story. Illustrated edition. Not been available since 1917, never before in paperback.

ISBN 1 872226 36 1 £4.95

## More Stories Of Old Lancashire
### (Frank Hird)
We present another 80 stories in the same easy, readable style, very enjoyable, great. With special section for Preston Guild 1992.

ISBN 1 872226 26 4 £4.95

## Stories & Tales Of Old Lancashire
### (Frank Hird)
Over 70 fascinating tales told in a wonderful light-hearted fashion. Witches, seiges and superstitions, battles and characters all here.

ISBN 1 872226 21 3 £4.95

## Poems & Songs Of Lancashire
### (Edwin Waugh)
A wonderful quality reprint of a classic book by undoubtedly one of Lancashire's finest poets. First published 1859 faithfully reproduced. Easy and pleasant reading, a piece of history.

ISBN 1 872226 27 2 £4.95

## The Best of Old Lancashire — Poetry & Verse
Published in 1866 as the very best of contemporary Lancashire writing, this book now offers a wonderful insight into the cream of Lancashire literature in the middle of the last century. Nearly 150 years later, edited and republished, the book now presents a unique opportunity to read again the masters of our past.

ISBN 1 872226 50 7 £4.95

## The Dock Road
### (J. Francis Hall RN)
A seafaring tale of old Liverpool. Set in the 1860s, with the American Civil War raging and the cotton famine gripping Lancashire. Period illustrations.

ISBN 1 872226 37 X £4.95

## The Lancashire Witches
### (W. Harrison Ainsworth)
A beautifully illustrated edition of the most famous romance of the supernatural.

ISBN 1 872226 55 8 £4.95

## Stories Of Great Lancastrians
### (written Frank Hird)
The lives of 24 great men of the county, told in easy reading style. Complete with sketches and drawings, a good introduction to the famous of Lancashire and Manchester. John Byrom, Arkwright, Tim Bobbins, Duke of Bridgewater.

ISBN 1 872226 23 X £4.95